D0527494

≞É CHONTAE ÁTHA CLIATH THEAS

rH DUBLIN COUNTY LIBRARIES

BALLYROAN BRANCH LIBRARY
TO RENEW ANY ITEM TEL: 494 1900
OR ONLINE AT www.southdublinlibraries.ie

be re

Withdrawn from Stock

Withdrawn from Stock

WOMEN PLAYWRIGHTS AT THE ABBEY 1904-2004

Edited and Introduced by
Colette Connor

HECUBA
2009

WOMEN PLAYWRIGHTS AT THE ABBEY 1904-2004
First Published in 2009 by

HECUBA
21 The Courtyard
St. Raphael's Manor
Celbridge
Co Kildare
IRELAND

Copywright © Colette Connor 1993, 2009

British Library Cataloguing in Publication Data
ISBN 978-0-9562325-0-2

Cover Design © IMAGO

Editor's Note

Grateful thanks to Women's Studies (WERRC) at University College, Dublin, where much of this research was carried out. Thanks also to my family and friends for their generous support over the years.

Colette Connor
May 2009

Contents

Introduction

When I first began work on this project, I made tentative enquiries as to the feasibility of finding out exactly how many women playwrights had work produced by the Abbey. If, for instance, the names, dates, and titles of the plays were already listed, then the object of the exercise was already self-defeating. What I found however, was exactly the opposite. No comprehensive listing of plays by women existed, not at the Abbey, not anywhere. The sad fact was that women playwrights had been so overshadowed by the mythology surrounding male playwrights at that august institution they had become virtually non-existent in historical terms.

Even the most cursory glance through any of the literature that deals with the Abbey from a historical standpoint will reveal that, apart from one or two well-known names like Lady Gregory or Teresa Deevy, the rest are hardly ever mentioned. Male playwrights, on the other hand, from major to positively minor, have had their work analysed and criticised ad nauseam. Numerous tomes treat of the works of Yeats, Synge and O'Casey, with countless references to Padraic Colum, George Fitzmaurice, Lennox Robinson, Paul Vincent Carroll, M.J. Molloy, Walter Macken and Louis D'Alton.

But where are the references to Winifred M. Letts, Katherine Francis Purdon, Susanne Day, Geraldine Cummins, Dorothy MacArdle, Mary Davenport O'Neill, Mairead Ni Ghrada, Mary Manning and Maura Laverty, to name but a few? Where are the articles and photographs, the biographies and life histories relating to these women? Search and you will search in vain. Until the reason for their neglect becomes all too clear: practically everything ever written that concerns our National Theatre and its achievements has been written from the male point of view.

The more one searches, the more one comes to realise that these women were far more significant in their own right than they have ever been given credit for, and yet the silence surrounding their existence has been deafening, not just because most people in Ireland have never heard of them, but because the Abbey itself has shamefully neglected them over the years.

To the best of my knowledge, not since the Abbey first opened its doors way back in 1904, has a retrospective of the work of women playwrights at the Abbey ever gone on view to the general public. Indeed, it is only in recent times that women who write for the stage have been taken seriously.

While male playwrights are busily engaged honing and crafting their masterpieces, women playwrights have had to find time to write in-between rearing and caring for their children and helping husbands to succeed in their chosen professions.

Even single women that write, unless they are possessed of independent means, must work in order to survive. To sit down and write a play, to think out a plot, can take anything up to two years in terms of personal commitment. In the meantime, who will mind the children, clean the house and cook the meals? And where is the money to come from to pay the bills once the writing gets underway?

So what does the future hold for women playwrights at the Abbey? Are we likely to see more plays by women produced on the Abbey stage, or less? And what is it that prevents plays by women from being staged in the first place?

To answer some of these questions, a worthwhile exercise might be to take a look back at those women who had work produced by the Abbey in the past.

As we look back over a hundred years of Abbey theatrical history, let us examine those women who have managed, despite the drawbacks, to have their work produced at the National Theatre.

The first and most obvious example is, of course, Lady Gregory, co-founder along with William Butler Yeats and John Millington Synge of the National Theatre Society. But even before Augusta Gregory came along, other women were already laying the groundwork for the national drama. Were it not for inspiration of Maud Gonne and Inghinidhe Na hEireann, there might never have been a National Theatre to begin with.

It was the coming together of this early group of feminists that led to the formation of the dramatic society from which the Fay Brothers and William Butler Yeats found the actors they needed to act out the roles in future plays. Indeed, it was the success of Alice Milligan's 1-Act melodrama 'The Last Feast of the Fianna' that inspired Yeats and Lady Gregory to produce further work. What they found however, was that there were very few plays to choose from, and so it was that Yeats and Lady Gregory set about the business of writing their own plays. It was Lady Gregory who helped Yeats to turn his play 'Cathleen Ni Houlihan' into a reality by helping him to put his dramatic fables into speech. She also supplied much of the dialogue and many of the plots and themes for his later work. She was equally generous with her talent when it came to helping other writers such as Douglas Hyde. And, in later years, both Synge and O'Casey would benefit greatly from her unstinting encouragement and advice.

The years 1902-1913, when she was between fifty and sixty years of age, found her at her most prolific. By the time she died in 1932 she had contributed an admirable total of thirty-six works to the Abbey repertoire. Her realistic prose plays proved immensely popular with the audiences of the day and, although in later years she may have been classified as a writer of simple peasant comedies, the fact remains that her output together with her fund-raising activities on behalf of the Abbey in the early years helped to keep that theatre afloat.

To achieve a more permanent home however, the National Theatre Society required more solid financial backing than even Lady Gregory was capable of providing, and so it was left to an Englishwoman, Annie Horniman, to step in and save the embryonic society from extinction. When Annie Horniman bought and paid for the old Mechanics Institute in Lower Abbey Street in 1904, she was to provide Ireland with its first and only National Theatre. To this day, however, the contribution Annie Horniman made towards the foundation of the National Theatre has never been fully acknowledged. Her name was omitted from the stone erected to honour the original founders and, apart from a portrait that hangs in the Abbey foyer, there is very little else on view to establish her link with that institution.

Following the inauguration of the Abbey in 1904, Augusta Gregory set to and began to pen a series of plays for presentation during the years 1904-1906, including 'Spreading the News', 'Kincora', 'The White Cockade' etc. In 1907, the first play to be produced at the Abbey by a woman other than Lady Gregory was 'The Eyes of the Blind' by Winifred M. Letts. Born in London in 1882, Winifred M. Letts was educated at Alexander College, Dublin. Following her marriage to V.H.F Verschoyle, Letts took up residence in Faversham, Kent, where she began to produce plays, poetry and short stories. One of these stories, 'The Challenge' was adapted for the Abbey stage in 1909. A 3-Act play 'Hamilton and Jones' was produced at the Gate Theatre in 1941. Winifred M. Letts died in 1950.

1913 saw the first production of 'The Homecoming' by Gertrude Robins and a 1-Act entitled 'My Lord' by Mrs Bart Kennedy. 'Broken Faith', a collaborative work by S.R. Day and G.D. Cummins was also presented. Susanne Rouvier Day and Geraldine Dorothy Cummins were early feminists who were actively involved in the women's movement of the time. Susanne Day wrote 'Women in the New Ireland' for the Munster Women's Franchise League and Geraldine Cummins wrote a biography of Dr. Edith Somerville.

Geraldine Cummins also wrote a collection of short stories entitled 'Variety Show' published in 1951. Another play, the 3-Act drama 'Fox and Geese' was produced by the Abbey in 1917.

1918 saw 'Aliens' by Rose McKenna and 'A Little Bit of Youth' by Christine Callister. On December 17th, Dorothy MacArdle's first play for the Abbey 'Atonement' was produced. Born in 1899 of Anglo-Irish stock, Dorothy MacArdle was educated at University College, Dublin, and taught at Alexander College. A staunch Republican and close friend of Eamon De Valera, she was active in the War of Independence. She also worked tirelessly on behalf of refugee children during World War II. It is impossible within the confines of this essay to do justice to all that MacArdle wrote. Suffice to say that her output in terms of plays, novels and short stories, screenplays and histories was, to say the least, prodigious. MacArdle's second play for the Abbey, 'Ann Kavanagh', produced in 1922, provided the Abbey actress May Craig one of her best loved and most popular roles and was revived several times. MacArdle's third play, 'The Old Man' was produced in 1925.

1919 'Brady' by Mrs Theodore Maynard.

1920: 'Candle and Crib' by K.F. Purdon. 'Candle and Crib' by Katherine Francis Purdon was published in book form by the Talbot Press in 1920. Handsomely produced and illustrated with colour plates by the artist Beatrice Elvery, the book is available for inspection at The National Library.

1926: 'Mr Murphy's Island' by Elizabeth Harte.

1927: 'Trifles' by Susan Glaspell.

1928: 'Full Measure' by Cathleen M. O'Brennan and 'The Woman' by Margaret O'Leary. In November 'The Women Have Their Way' by Helen Granville-Barker was brought in as an independent production.

1930 saw a production of Teresa Deevy's first play 'The Reapers' at the Abbey. This was followed in 1931 with a one-act entitled 'The Disciple'. In 1932, Deevy's third play, 'Temporal Powers', was joint prize-winner with 'Things That Are Caesar's' by Paul Vincent Carroll. Deevy followed this success in 1935 with 'The King of Spain's Daughter' and in 1936 her best-loved play 'Katie Roche' was produced and revived several times thereafter by the Abbey. Another of her plays, 'The Wild Goose' was staged in November of that year.

Born in Waterford January 21st, 1894, Teresa Deevy had her first success with a play for BBC Radio. For a woman who first knew deafness in her early teens and who did not begin to write plays until after she was totally deaf, her achievement is all the more remarkable. Able to speak and lip-read French fluently, Deevy travelled extensively on the continent, often acting as a brancardiere during her annual visits to Lourdes. After the death of her sister, to whom she was closely attached, Deevy retired to a nursing home where she died on January 19th 1963.

Although Teresa Deevy's plays might well be regarded as being somewhat dated today, they still retain a feel for dialogue that is natural, honest and direct in its appeal. In all, Teresa Deevy wrote six plays for the Abbey, and proved to be an outstanding box-office success.

1931: 'Winning Ways' by Helen Staunton produced by Essandee Productions played for one week. Set in the dining-room of a Dublin home, it has a cast of four males and five females. The Producer was Dorothy Day.

Belfast Rep presented 'The Land of the Stranger' by Dorothea Down Byrne. This play, an Ulster-American comedy, is set in a New York shop/Ulster kitchen, and has a cast of seven males and five females.

1935: 'Summer's Day' by Maura Molloy.

1936: 'Wind from the West' by Maeve O'Callaghan.

1937: 'Who Will Remember....?' by Maura Molloy dealt with the decline of the Anglo-Irish Ascendency. This was followed by 'The Patriot', Maeve O'Callaghan's second play for the Abbey.

By now it was possible to see the influential hand of the newly-appointed Managing Director at the Abbey, Ernest Blyth. Blyth, an Ulster Protestant who travelled to the South to become Minister for Finance in the Free State Government, combined his love for the Irish language with his life-long love affair with the Abbey, an affair that lasted for almost forty years.

1938: 'Pilgrims' by Mary Rynne.

1940: 'Mount Prospect' by Elizabeth Connor, 'The Birth of a Giant' by Nora McAdam and 'Three to Go' by Olga Fielden. 'Mount Prospect' by Elizabeth Connor, another prize-winner at the Abbey, was adapted from a novel of the same name. Connor followed this in 1941 with 'Swans and Geese'.

In 1942, Connor's third play, 'An Apple a Day' was produced. This three-act comedy, set in the living-room of a dispensary house in the fictional Carrigmahon, has a cast of eleven, six males, five females. Another of Connor's plays, 'The Dark Road' ran for six weeks in 1947.

1943: 'Poor Man's Miracle' by Marian Hemar.

1944: 'Laistiar D'en Eadan' by Eibhlin Ni Shuilleabhan is set in a house/kitchen and has a cast of three males and three females.

'The Coloured Balloon' by Margaret O'Leary, a 3-Act Comedy, was produced in November of that year with a cast of four males and seven females.

1945 ushered in Mairead Ni Ghrada's first play for the Abbey 'Giolla an Tsoluis'.

1948: J.M. Barrie's play ' Mary Rose' received an Irish translation by Siobhan Ni Chionaith (the actress Siobhan McKenna) under the title 'Maire Ros'.

Two other plays in Irish, 'Na Cloigini' by Maighread Nic Mhaicin and 'Bean and Mhi-Ghra' by Padraigin Ni Neill were also staged.

Many of the plays written by women and produced by the Abbey at this time were directed by Frank Dermody. Dermody came to the Abbey originally from An Taibhdhearc in Galway, and his greatest achievement on behalf of women playwrights was his production of 'An Triail' by Mairead Ni Ghrada for the 1964 Dublin Theatre Festival. 'An Triail', twenty years ahead of its time in terms of subject matter – the trial by jury (the audience) of a young unmarried mother who has committed infanticide – was the hit of the Festival that year and went on to achieve a long and successful run.

When the Abbey was destroyed by fire in July 1951, the old Queen's Theatre in Pearse Street was leased until such time as the new Abbey could be erected on the site of the old. In the event, the company was to remain at the Queen's for some fifteen years. The theatre, which had a seating capacity of 760 - double that of the Abbey - proved difficult to fill. Ernest Blyth, in his determination to keep the Abbey going, was prepared to forsake quality in favour of quantity at the box-office. In consequence, only safe plays were produced and the result was dead theatre. However, it is unlikely that the Abbey would have survived had it not been for Blyth's intervention, and there is no doubt that his instincts for the Abbey's survival at this time helped save the National Theatre from extinction.

'Window on the Square' by Anne Daly was the first play by a woman playwright into the Queen's in 1951. The production was directed by Ria Mooney. Ria Mooney joined the Abbey in 1924 along with the actress Sheelah Richards.

Sheelah Richards, later married the playwright Denis Johnston, and went on to produce and direct with her own company at the Olympia Theatre, managing at the same time to produce a daughter, the well-known novelist and playwright Jennifer Johnston.

When Ria Mooney took charge of the Abbey School of Acting in 1936, her work with young actors led on to the Experimental Theatre at the Peacock. Here the work of new playwrights was tried out, among them Teresa Deevy and Mary Davenport O'Neill. Whether Mary Davenport O'Neill ever had a play produced by the Abbey is uncertain, but certainly her work was performed on the experimental stage of the Peacock.

A friend of Yeats, Mary Davenport O'Neill was born in Dublin in 1879 and later went on to study at the National College of Art in Kildare Street. Married to Joseph O'Neill, she was the author of many plays and a poetry collection 'Prometheus and Other Poems' was also published. Her verse play 'Bluebeard' was produced by Austin Clarke's Lyric Theatre in 1933, and another of her plays 'Cain' in 1945.

Ria Mooney left the Abbey in 1943 to direct at the Gaiety, but returned again in 1948. The years spent at the Queen's proved an unhappy experience for the talented Miss Mooney who became worn down by the lack of colour in many the plays she was expected to produce. Following a nervous breakdown in 1962 she was forced to resign from the company. Ria Mooney died in 1973, after years of faithful service given over to the Abbey.

1953: 'La Bui Bealtaine' by Mairead Ni Ghrada.

1955: 'The Last Move' by Pauline Maguire. This was followed in November by another Ni Ghrada play 'Ull Glas Oiche Shamhna'.

1958: 'Ar Buille a Hoct' (A Knock at Eight) by Majorie Watson, and 'An Strainsear' (The Stranger)

1959: 'Leave It To The Doctor' by Anne Daly, her second play at the Queen's. 'Sugan Sneachta' by Mairead Ni Ghrada. Ni Ghrada followed this in 1960 with her fourth play 'Mac Ui Rudai'.

1961: 'The Good and Obedient Young Man' by Betty Barr translated as 'An Fear Og Umhal Malda' by Eoin O'Suilleabhain.

1964:   'Liffey Lane' by Maura Laverty was brought in as an independent production by the amateur dramatic group Cairde Fail Players. Laverty's plays were slices of life from the Dublin slums of the time.

'A Page of History' by Eilis Dillon was the last play by a woman playwright to be staged at the Queen's. The action of the play revolves around two sisters who have fallen on hard times and can no longer afford the upkeep of the 'Big House'. Dillon, with a long list of novels to her credit, was also the author of many children's books. A former Chairman of the Irish Writer's Union and a member of Aosdana, Eilis Dillon died in 1994.

With the opening of the new Abbey on the site of the old in 1966, we witness a new development as regards plays by women. Increasingly, we find that more and more plays are being produced at the Peacock Theatre rather than on the main stage of the Abbey. In a programme note penned for the opening of the Experimental Theatre at the Peacock Theatre back in 1937, Ria Mooney gives the reasons for the establishment of that theatre. *'...for the production of plays by Irish authors whose work was considered not suitable or not sufficiently advanced technically for production on the Abbey stage, and yet was of sufficient high standard to merit public presentation.'*

Reading this one has to conclude that, consciously or unconsciously, the work of women playwrights was no longer considered 'finished work.' At the same time however, plays mounted on the Abbey stage at this time are overwhelmingly the work of male playwrights. Apart from Edna O'Brien, Mary Manning and Teresa Deevy, no other plays by women were produced by the Abbey at this time, although an increase in the number of plays written by women and presented at the Peacock is noticeable from the late 1960s' onwards.

1968: 'Breithiuntas' by Mairead Ni Ghrada was produced on the Peacock stage while over at the Abbey Mary Manning's adaptation of Frank O'Connor's story 'The Saint and Mary Kate' was filling seats. Manning, a drama critic with Hibernia, wrote many plays, including 'Youth's The Season'. She also adapted Joyce's 'Finnegan's Wake' under the title 'The Voice of Shem'.

1969: 'The Butterfly Who Couldn't Dance' by Maire Holmes, directed by Nuala Hayes is produced at the Peacock.

1970: Audrey Welsh, married to the Irish actor John Welsh of 'Forsyth Saga' fame, adapted Flann O'Brien's satirical novel 'At Swim Two Birds' for the Peacock stage.

1971:   'Ulysses in Nighttown' by Majorie Barkentine is produced in August of that year.

1971 also saw the appointment of Lelia Doolan as Artistic Director at the Abbey. Doolan, who resigned from RTE as a Producer following an acrimonious and much publicised dispute over broadcasting standards, was appointed in place of Hugh Hunt.

As always with the National Theatre however, the idealism of the new Artistic Director was soon to clash with the more entrenched position of the Abbey's Board of Directors. The new Artistic Director's tenure proved of short duration, her appointment ending after little more than a year. Away from the National Theatre environment however, Doolin became productive once more, this time in the world of film, spreading her wings in the West of Ireland where she felt the real nucleus of artistic creativity was taking place.

1973: 'A Doll in the Gap' by Helen Cahill, 'Rites' by Maureen Duffy and 'Coats' by Lady Gregory.

1974: Majorie Barkentine's 'Ulysses in Nighttown' transferred from the Peacock to the Abbey stage.

In October 1974, Edna O'Brien's second play 'The Gathering' was produced. Although it received much hostile criticism from a hostile press at the time, 'The Gathering' nevertheless went on to gross the highest week's box-office takings for any play in the history of the Abbey.

1975 brought in a new production of Teresa Deevy's 'Katie Roche' while over in the Peacock the Sundrive Players produced Mary Manning's 'The Voice of Shem' - first prize-winner in the All-Ireland Amateur Drama Festival that year.

1976: 'Mothers' by May Cluskey - a one-woman show written for the Peacock stage by the former Abbey actress. In December 'End of Term' by Maeve Binchy was also produced at the Peacock.

1977: Edna O'Brien's third play for the Abbey, 'A Pagan Place' was produced. Once again it brought the usual vitriolic criticism from the press although John Finegan of the Evening Herald found it: *'A compassionate and in the final moments particularly, a very moving play'.*

1978: 'The Heart's a Wonder' by Maureen Charlton.

1979: 'The Nightingale and Not the Lark' by Jennifer Johnston centred on the lives of her actress mother Sheelah Richards and her playwright father Denis Johnston.

1979: Maeve Binchy's second play for the Peacock 'Half-Promised Land' was produced.

'Open-Ended Prescription' by Leland Bardwell opened at the Peacock on September 11[th.]

1981: a second production for Eilis Dillon – 'The Cat's Opera' – for which Dillon wrote both the music and the lyrics.

1982: 'Mary Makebelieve', a musical based on 'The Charwoman's Daughter' by James Stephens, was adapted for the Peacock stage by husband and wife team Fergus and Rosaleen Linehan.

1983: 'Sylvia Plath - Letters Home' based on the correspondence between Plath and her mother, was dramatised for the stage by Rose Goldenberg.

'Chocolate Sauce' by Mary Gallagher was produced at the Peacock in May of that year.

1984: A programme of 'Prose and Poetry' was produced by Niamh McAnally, daughter of the Abbey actor Ray McAnally.

'Crimes of the Heart' by Beth Hanley was staged at the Peacock in March. In May, Anne Hartigan's play 'I Do Like to be Beside the Seaside' received a staged reading at the Peacock.

1984: 'Cuirt An Mhean Oiche' (The Midnight Court) adapted for the stage by Siobhan McKenna followed in October.

1985: In January 'Freud' by Lynn Roth. Then in June, four Irish plays ran for two weeks: 'Leamh Filiochta' by Aine Ni Ghlinn. 'Na Boghaisini Go Brach' by Poilin McGonigle. 'An Fear Siuil' by Lady Gregory and 'Agallamh Beirte Ta's Agam' by Mairead MacIomaire.

1986: 'Or By Appointment', May Cluskey's second play for the Peacock.

1987: Carolyn Swift's play 'Lady G', based on the life of Lady Gregory, was produced at the Peacock with the actress Maire O'Neill in the leading role. A one-time member of the Abbey's Board of Directors, Swift was also the founder with her partner Alan Simpson of the Pike Theatre in Herbert Lane Dublin in 1953. Swift's book "Stage By Stage" describes the triumphs and tribulations of life at The Pike during those early years.

In September 1987, a new play by Jennifer Johnston 'The Invisible Man' was produced at the Peacock to good notices.

1987: In December, Charabanc, a women's theatre group from Northern Ireland, brought its production of 'Somewhere over the Balcony' by Marie Jones to the Peacock. The play, which examined with insight the lives of women living in the Divis Flats area of Belfast, was warmly received by both audiences and critics.

1988 saw 'Shady Ladies' by Mary Halpin at the Peacock. Halpin, a storyline editor for the RTE series 'Fair City', won the 1982 Irish Times Woman Playwright Competition with her play 'Semi-Private'.

For the 1988 Dublin Theatre Festival the Abbey staged a new play 'Colours' by Jean Binnie. 'Colours' set between 1806 and 1865 tells the story of Dr Jane Barry Esquire who disguised herself as a man in order to gain admittance into the British Army as a medical doctor. 'Colours' produced a cast of eighteen actors performing forty-three different roles. Despite excellent performances and a splendid setting, the play received a lukewarm reception from both audiences and critics. 'Colours' is an important landmark however in that it was to signal the last play by a woman playwright to be produced on the main stage of the Abbey for over a decade.

Karen Sunde's play 'Dark Lady' was staged at the Peacock in November. Jennifer Johnston's play, 'O Ananias, Azarias and Misael', her third for the Peacock, was also staged in November of that year.

1989: 'Fragments of Isabella' by Isabella Leitner. 'Triptych' by Jennifer Johnston and 'Shades of the Jelly Woman' by Jean Doyle, developed for the Peacock stage by the writer and director Peter Sheridan.

In 1989, five women playwrights, Ivy Bannister, Leland Bardwell, Celia De Freine Clairr O'Connor and Colette Connor came together with an Administrator Phyl Herbert to form the Women Playwrights' Forum. The objective: to apply to the Arts Council of Ireland for funding under the 1990 Theatre Project Award Scheme.

Grant-aid was sought for the work-shopping of five plays, followed by a rehearsed reading of each play. A special grant of £2,000 was subsequently awarded on the basis of the women's assertion that:

'A public performance for any playwright is difficult, but for women playwrights it would appear to be almost impossible.'

When news of the award was received, all five women met with the Administrator to discuss future plans for the project. Having received the grant they now felt it imperative that five women directors be appointed to workshop the plays, select the actors and direct the readings. In the weeks that followed, various venues were discussed where those readings might take place. As it happened, the granting of the award that year coincided with the appointment of Garry Hynes as Artistic Director at the Abbey. Hynes had brought journalist and critic Fintan O'Toole onboard as Literary Advisor and so it was decided that O'Toole should be approached with a view to having the readings staged at the Peacock. A meeting between Herbert and O'Toole followed during which it was agreed that all five scripts should be submitted for consideration. Early in 1991, the Abbey came back with its decision. For one week only from June 24th to 29th 1991 a series of rehearsed readings of 'Plays by Women' were to be presented at the Peacock.

1991: Marina Carr's play 'Ullaloo' was produced on the Peacock stage in March of that year. This absurdist Beckettian type drama was directed by David Byrne.

.

1991: June 24th to 29th, a series of 'Plays by Women' receives Rehearsed Readings at the Peacock. The first three plays, staged for two evenings each were:

'The Wilde Circus Show' by Ivy Bannister
Directed by Mary Elizabeth Burke-Kennedy

'Find the Lady' by Louise Hermana
Directed by Pat Murphy

'Dervorgilla and Hyacinth Halvey'
by Lady Gregory - Directed by Judy Friel

On Saturday, June 29th, 1991, the Abbey, in association with the Women Playwright's Forum, presents a further series of Rehearsed Readings:

'Generations' by Colette Connor
Directed by Claire Wilson

'Bodies' by Clairr O'Connor
Directed by Cathy Leeney

'Two Girls in Silk Kimonos' by Celia De Freine
Directed by Maire O'Higgins

'Jocasta' by Leland Bardwell
Directed by Mia Gallagher

'The Rebel Countess' by Ivy Bannister
Directed by Caroline Fitzgerald

A discussion followed the readings. Chaired by Phyl Herbert of the Women Playwrights Forum and attended by Garry Hynes, the discussion centred on the reasons why so many of the plays written by women failed to make it to the full production stage at the Abbey. The debate that followed showed those present firmly united in the belief that the National Theatre needed to be much more proactive on behalf of women playwrights if women's voices were to be heard. In response, Hynes said the present series of 'Plays by Women' was just part of 'a range of artillery' the Abbey hoped to deploy in the future in relation to all kinds of work. Two years later however, Hynes resigned her position as Artistic Director and so whatever hopes and aspirations those present on the day may have entertained as regards the future for women playwrights those hopes and aspirations no longer applied to the Abbey. None of the plays that received rehearsed readings in 1991 went on to receive full productions. If the work of Lady Gregory is excluded, that means that of the seven plays presented that week, only one was considered worthy of further examination. That left six plays without further workshops or further assistance once the readings came to an end. A charge often laid at the Abbey's door in the past is that it has rejected a great deal of good work while managing to produce a lot of work that is very obviously bad. That charge still holds good today.

Despite the fact that the National Theatre defends its system of play selection, there are times when the logic behind that selection is difficult to fathom. All too often it seems as if mediocrity is rewarded with the work of established playwrights being accepted for production – work that all too often receives less than favourable reviews and plays to half-empty houses – while strong and interesting work by women playwrights is rejected.

Of course, new plays by women *are* produced at the Peacock from time to time but usually only after the work has managed to prove itself elsewhere. This applies to at least three plays staged at the Peacock between 1990 and 1992.

'Howling Moons, Silent Sons' by Deirdre Hines which focused on incestuous family relationships, transferred to the Peacock following a successful production mounted by Pigsback Theatre Company at the Project during the 1991 Dublin Theatre Festival.

'Away Alone' by Janet Noble which examines the problems facing young Irish-American immigrants, was brought in from New York where it played to enthusiastic audiences at the Irish Centre.

'Bold Girls' by the Scottish playwright Rona Monro, set in Northern Ireland and centering on the betrayal of wives by husbands, was already a critically well-received production before being taken on board at the Peacock.

Following the series of rehearsed readings of 'Plays By Women' in 1991, women playwrights disappeared off the radar for a time where the Abbey was concerned and it was left to independent theatre companies to carry on the chant of 'There Are No Women Playwrights.'

The year 1993 was a fallow year for women playwrights at the Abbey. Towards the end of 1994 however, another flurry of activity took place.

1994: 'The Wall' by Ivy Bannister received a rehearsed reading at the Peacock.

1994: In September of that year Marina Carr's new play 'The Mai' directed by Garry Hynes was produced on the Peacock stage. With the help of Hynes, Carr had worked closely on the play over a two-year period. Leaving aside her absurdist leanings, Carr now focussed her attention on the lives of an Irish family as seen through the lens of four generations. The combustible result showed what could be achieved when a woman playwright and a woman director come together to collaborate.

'The Mai' was a resounding success and went on to establish Carr as a new and exciting voice in Irish theatre. 'The Mai' also marked a sea-change in Carr's work for the stage.

'Dun na mBan Tri Thine' by Eilis Ni Dhuibhne produced by Amharclann de hide is staged at the Peacock in November of that year.

1995: 'Small City' by Clare Dowling received a lunchtime production at the Peacock in May. 'Playgirl' by Katy Hayes followed in October of the same year. Founders of Groundwork Productions with their production of 'There Are No Women Playwrights' Parts I & II, Dowling and Hayes were finally rewarded in having their own work produced at the Abbey.

1996: Marina Carr's second play 'Portia Coughlan' directed by Garry Hynes is staged at the Peacock.

In May 'A Wing and A Prayer' was delivered by The Balcony Belles, a women's theatre group from the Liberties in Dublin, formed originally as part of a Community project.

1997: 'A Different Rhythm' by Lorraine O'Brien, was produced at the Peacock after having first established itself as Theatre in the Community.

1998: 'By the Bog of Cats', Marina Carr's third play to be produced by the National Theatre and the first play written by a woman to appear on the main stage of the Abbey since Jean Binnie's play 'Colours' was produced as part of the 1988 Dublin Theatre Festival.

2000: 'Tree Houses' by Elizabeth Kuti is produced at the Peacock in April.

2001: 'The Memory of Water' by Shelagh Stephenson is staged in May.

2002: Rehearsed Readings of 'Doldrum Bay' by Hilary Fannin on August 16th and 'Lovers Reunited' by Siofra Campbell on August 17th at the Peacock.

2002: Marina Carr's 'Ariel' is produced on the Abbey stage.

2003: 'Meat and Salt' by Marina Carr (as part of the 'Sons and Daughters' project in collaboration with Jim Nolan of Red Kettle Theatre Company) is staged at the Peacock.

'Doldrum Bay' by Hilary Fannin (which received a rehearsed reading in August 2002), receives a full production at the Peacock in May.

2003: In December of that year, Paula Meehan's play 'The Wolf of Winter' is produced on the Peacock stage.

2004: 'Portia Coughlan' by Marina Carr is revived at the Peacock.

It is now twenty years since a woman playwright, other than Marina Carr, had her work produced on the main stage of the Abbey. In this country, it is not fashionable to criticise national institutions. There is a feeling that in doing so, one is being disloyal to one's own. This is especially true in the case of the Abbey. As the National Theatre it has enjoyed enormous success both at home and abroad with its many stirring and indigenous productions helping to enhance Ireland's reputation around the world. But sometimes criticism is necessary and sometimes it is justified, particularly when the intention is not to damage, but rather to draw attention to the latent inequality that lies at the heart of the Abbey's artistic policy. For the plain fact is that in this country the National Theatre does very little for women playwrights.

It is all very well for Abbey Management to say they are aware of the problem but if they are aware of the problem then it is time they did something positive to resolve it. Announcing every now and then that a further series of 'Plays by Women' are to receive rehearsed readings is not the answer. Twenty or thirty minute readings of new plays are worthless unless they are followed up by workshops and rehearsals leading to full productions.

One dislikes having to hark back to Marina Carr, but the fact is, no other woman playwright has enjoyed so much unparalleled success as Carr has enjoyed at the Abbey. No-one disputes that Carr is an exceptional playwright – she has proved her credentials over and over again. However, the fact that Ireland has managed to produce one women playwright of outstanding merit and placed her on the international stage does not mean that other women playwrights should be neglected in her favour. As an exceptional playwright, Carr has done exceptionally well, but it is time other women's voices were heard.

It is erroneous to suggest that women are not writing plays. Women are very definitely writing plays – the problem is those plays are not being produced.

Perhaps one reason for this is that women in this country have never had access to the purse-strings in the same way as their male counterparts. All too often funding and sponsorship has come in the form of piecemeal payments and usually only after a long and time-consuming struggle during which plays that might have been produced have been left to languish through lack of encouragement and/or support. The Arts Council has a role to play here. Women working outside the Abbey lack the kind of workshop/rehearsal/production facilities that are required to lift the work from the page into the mouths of actors and place it onstage where it belongs. One way of tackling the problem would be to institute an Experimental Theatre Workshop of the kind that Ria Mooney was engaged with when she was in situ at the Abbey. Not only would this provide a necessary space where women playwrights could try out new work, it would also be a way of paying homage to Mooney who gave so much of her time and energy over to the solving of problems in relation to the work of playwrights. Anyone who understands the business of theatre understands that for a play to be given life it first has to be seen and heard. Garry Hynes has already gone on record to point this out: *'The hard fact is that a play has no existence in and of itself. It is nothing until it is imagined, that is, performed.'*

Throughout its history the Abbey has produced great work by great women, women who have struggled against the odds to achieve and pass on the benefits of that achievement to the generations of women coming after them. The ghosts of those women walk beside us as a reminder that there is work still to be done. A reminder of what can be achieved once the will to achieve is there. The evidence for this is to be found in the many plays by women produced during the years when Yeats and Lady Gregory held sway, and even at the Queen's during Ernest Blyth's tenure and most certainly throughout the 1970s and 1980s at the Peacock, the number of plays by women that were produced then is remarkable when one considers the small amount of plays written by women that the Abbey produces today. The fact is until such time as women playwrights are allowed to succeed or fail in the same way as their male counterparts, no change in the present status quo is possible. Women playwrights with new, vibrant voices are waiting to be heard. If we fail to hear them, we fail in our duty to all those women who fought so long and so hard to have their work presented on the Abbey stage.

Let us hope the Abbey is listening.

Colette Connor
May 2009

CHRONOLOGY

WOMEN PLAYWRIGHTS AT THE ABBEY 1904-2004

YEAR	VENUE	DATE	TITLE	PLAYWRIGHT
1904	ABBEY	DEC 27	SPREADING THE NEWS	LADY GREGORY
1905	ABBEY	MAR 25	KINCORA	LADY GREGORY
1905	ABBEY	DEC 9	THE WHITE COCKADE	LADY GREGORY
1906	ABBEY	FEB 19	HYACINTH HALVEY	LADY GREGORY
1906	ABBEY	MAR16	THE DOCTOR IN SPITE OF HIMSELF	MOLIERE/ GREGORY
1906	ABBEY	OCT 20	THE GAOL GATE	LADY GREGORY
1906	ABBEY	DEC 8	THE CANAVANS	LADY GREGORY
1907	ABBEY	FEB 23	THE JACKDAW	LADY GREGORY
1907	ABBEY	MAR 9	THE RISING OF THE MOON	LADY GREGORY
1907	ABBEY	APR 1	THE EYES OF THE BLIND	WINIFRED M. LETTS
1907	ABBEY	APR 3	THE POORHOUSE	GREGORY/D.HYDE
1907	ABBEY	SEP 30	DEVORGILLA	LADY GREGORY
1908	ABBEY	MAR 9	TEJA	H.SUDERMANN/ GREGORY
1908	ABBEY	APR 4	THE ROGUERIES OF SCAPIN	MOLIERE/GREGORY
1908	ABBEY	APR 20	THE WORKHOUSE WARD	LADY GREGORY
1909	ABBEY	JAN 21	THE MISER	MOLIERE/GREGORY
1909	ABBEY	OCT 14	THE CHALLENGE	WINIFRED M. LETTS
1909	ABBEY	NOV 11	THE IMAGE	LADY GREGORY
1910	ABBEY	FEB 24	MIRANDOLINA	GOLDINI/GREGORY
1910	ABBEY	MAR 2	THE TRAVELLING MAN	LADY GREGORY
1910	ABBEY	NOV 10	THE FULL MOON	LADY GREGORY
1910	ABBEY	DEC 1	COATS	LADY GREGORY
1911	ABBEY	JAN 5	THE NATIVITY	GREGORY/D.HYDE
1911	ABBEY	JAN 12	THE DELIVERER	LADY GREGORY

YEAR	VENUE	DATE	TITLE	PLAYWRIGHT
1912	ABBEY	JAN 11	MACDONOUGH'S WIFE	LADY GREGORY
1912	ABBEY	JUL 4	THE BOGIE MAN	LADY GREGORY
1912	ABBEY	NOV 21	DAMER'S GOLD	LADY GREGORY
1913	ABBEY	APR 10	THE HOMECOMING	GERTRUDE ROBINS
1913	ABBEY	APR 24	BROKEN FAITH	SUSANNE ROUVIER DAY & GERALDINE CUMMINS
1913	ABBEY	OCT 16	MY LORD	MRS BART KENNEDY
1914	ABBEY	JAN 27	THE CANAVANS	LADY GREGORY
1915	ABBEY	APR 8	SHANWALLA	LADY GREGORY
1916	ABBEY	-	-	-
1917	ABBEY	FEB 2	FOX AND GEESE	SUSANNE ROUVIER DAY & GERALDINE CUMMINS
1918	ABBEY	JAN 29	HANRAHAN'S OATH	LADY GREGORY
1918	ABBEY	MAR 12	ALIENS	ROSE MCKENNA
1918	ABBEY	MAY 28	A LITTLE BIT OF YOUTH	CHRISTINE MCALLISTER
1918	ABBEY	DEC 17	ATTONEMENT	DOROTHY MACARDLE
1919	ABBEY	APR 21	THE DRAGON	LADY GREGORY
1919	ABBEY	AUG 4	BRADY	MRS THEODORE MAYNARD
1920	ABBEY	JAN 6	THE GOLDEN APPLE	LADY GREGORY
1920	ABBEY	DEC 20	CANDLE AND CRIB	KATHERINE FRANCIS PURDON
1921	ABBEY	AUG 8	ARISTOTLE'S BELLOWS	LADY GREGORY
1922	ABBEY	APR 6	ANN KAVANAGH	DOROTHY MACARDLE
1923	ABBEY	DEC 31	THE OLD WOMAN REMEMBERS	LADY GREGORY
1924	ABBEY	JAN 15	THE PERFECT DAY	UNKNOWN
1924	ABBEY	APR 14	THE STORY BROUGHT BY BRIGIT	LADY GREGORY

YEAR	VENUE	DATE	TITLE	PLAYWRIGHT
1925	ABBEY	FEB 24	THE OLD MAN	DOROTHY MACARDLE
1926	ABBEY	JAN 4	THE WOULD-BE GENTLEMAN	MOLIERE/GREGORY
1926	ABBEY	APR 16	MR MURPHY'S ISLAND	ELIZABETH HARTE
1927	ABBEY	JAN 24	TRIFLES	SUSAN GLASPELL
1927	ABBEY	MAR 14	SANCHO'S MASTER	LADY GREGORY
1927	ABBEY	MAY 9	DAVE	LADY GREGORY
1928	ABBEY	AUG 27	FULL MEASURE	CATHLEEN M. O'BRENNAN
1928	ABBEY	SEP10	THE WOMAN	MARGARET O'LEARY
1928	ABBEY	NOV 12	THE WOMEN HAVE THEIR WAY	HELEN GRANVILLE-BARKER
1930	ABBEY	MAR 18	THE REAPERS	TERESA DEEVY
1931	ABBEY	AUG 24	A DISCIPLE	TERESA DEEVY
1931	ABBEY	NOV 16	WINNING WAYS	HELEN STAUNTON
1931	ABBEY	NOV 30	THE LAND OF THE STRANGER	DOROTHEA DOWN BYRNE
1932	ABBEY	SEP 12	TEMPORAL POWERS	TERESA DEEVY
1933	ABBEY	JUL 25	BLUEBEARD	MARY DAVENPORT O'NEILL
1934	ABBEY	DEC 10	THE CANAVANS	LADY GREGORY
1935	ABBEY	APR 29	THE KING OF SPAIN'S DAUGHTER	TERESA DEEVY
1935	ABBEY	DEC 9	SUMMER'S DAY	MAURA MOLLOY
1936	ABBEY	MAR 16	KATIE ROCHE	TERESA DEEVY
1936	ABBEY	NOV 9	THE WILD GOOSE	TERESA DEEVY
1936	ABBEY	NOV 30	WIND FROM THE WEST	MAEVE O'CALLAGHAN
1937	ABBEY	MAY 17	WHO WILL REMEMBER...?	MAURA MOLLOY
1937	ABBEY	AUG 5	THE PATRIOT	MAEVE O'CALLAGHAN
1938	ABBEY	OCT 10	PILGRIMS	MARY RYNNE

YEAR	VENUE	DATE	TITLE	PLAYWRIGHT
1940	ABBEY	APR 22	MOUNT PROSPECT	ELIZABETH CONNOR
1940	ABBEY	MAY 13	THE BIRTH OF A GIANT	NORA MACADAM
1940	ABBEY	NOV 4	THREE TO GO	OLGA FIELDEN
1941	ABBEY	SEP 22	SWANS AND GEESE	ELIZABETH CONNOR
1942	ABBEY	SEP 7	AN APPLE A DAY	ELIZABETH CONNOR
1943	ABBEY	DEC 27	POOR MAN'S MIRACLE	MARIAN HEMAR/ F.B. CZARNOMSKI
1944	ABBEY	JAN 30	LAISTIER D'EN EADAN	EIBHLIN NI SHUILLEABHAIN
1944	ABBEY	MAY 8	THE COLOURED BALLOON	MARGARET O'LEARY
1945	ABBEY	MAR 18	GIOLLA AN TSOLUIS	MAIREAD NI GHRADA
1946	ABBEY	NOV 15	CARA AN PHOBAIL	LADY GREGORY
1947	ABBEY	MAY 12	THE DARK ROAD	ELIZABETH CONNOR
1948	ABBEY	MAR 16	MAIRE ROS (MARY ROSE)	SIOBHAN NIC CHIONAITH/J.M.BARRIE
1948	ABBEY	OCT 11	NA CLOIGINI	MAIGHREAD NI MHAICIN
1949	ABBEY	OCT 31	BEAN AN MHI-GHRA (LA MALQUERIDA)	PADRAIGIN NI NEILL (JACINTA BENAVENTE)
1950	ABBEY	-	-	-
1951	QUEENS	OCT 22	WINDOW ON THE SQUARE	ANNE DALY
1952	QUEENS	MAY 26	THE APPLE TREE	LADY GREGORY
1952	QUEENS	OCT 11	EIRI NA GEALAI	LADY GREGORY
1953	QUEENS	NOV 1	LA BUI BEALTAINE	MAIREAD NI GHRADA
1954	QUEENS	-	-	-
1955	QUEENS	OCT 24	THE LAST MOVE	PAULINE MAGUIRE
1955	QUEENS	NOV 5	ULL GLAS OICHE SHAMHRA	MAIREAD NI GHRADA
1956	QUEENS	-	-	-
1957	QUEENS	-	-	-

YEAR	VENUE	DATE	TITLE	PLAYWRIGHT
1958	QUEENS	JUL 15	AR BUILLE A HOCT (A KNOCK AT EIGHT)	MAJORIE WATSON
1958	QUEENS	NOV 17	AN STRAINSEAR	UNKNOWN
1959	QUEENS	SEP 14	LEAVE IT TO THE DOCTOR	ANNE DALY
1959	QUEENS	SEP 29	SUGAN SNEACHTA	MAIREAD NI GHRADA
1960	QUEENS	NOV 13	THE GOOD AND OBEDIENT YOUNG MAN	BETTY BARR/EOIN O'SUILLEABHAIN
1961	QUEENS	-	-	-
1962	QUEENS	-	-	-
1964	QUEENS	APR 27	LIFFEY LANE	MAURA LAVERTY
1964	QUEENS	NOV 23	A PAGE OF HISTORY	EILIS DILLON
1965	QUEENS			
1966	QUEENS	MAY 23	GEATA AN PHRIOSUIN	LADY GREGORY
1967	QUEENS	OCT 5	A BRECHT EVENING	AGNES BERNELLE
1968	PEACOCK	FEB 5	BREITHIUNTAS	MAIREAD NI GHRADA
1968	ABBEY	MAR 18	THE SAINT AND MARY KATE	MARY MANNING/ FRANK O'CONNOR
1969	PEACOCK	MAR 31	THE WAKEFIELD MYSTERY PLAYS	SALLY MILES
1970	PEACOCK	FEB 12	AT SWIM TWO BIRDS	AUDREY WELSH/ FLANN O'BRIEN
1971	PEACOCK	AUG 31	ULYSSES IN NIGHTTOWN	MARJORIE BARKENTINE
1972	PEACOCK	-	-	-
1973	PEACOCK	FEB 26	A DOLL IN THE GAP	HELEN CAHILL
1973	PEACOCK	MAR 19	RITES	MAUREEN DUFFY
1973	PEACOCK	JUL 30	COATS	LADY GREGORY
1973	PEACOCK	NOV 11	ONCE IN ANOTHER WORLD	HEDLI MACNEICE

YEAR	VENUE	DATE	TITLE	PLAYWRIGHT
1974	ABBEY	JUL 15	ULYSSES IN NIGHTTOWN	MARJORIE BERKENTINE
1974	ABBEY	OCT 9	THE GATHERING	EDNA O'BRIEN
1975	ABBEY	JUN 2	KATIE ROCHE	TERESA DEEVY
1976	PEACOCK	JAN 29	MOTHERS	MAY CLUSKEY
1976	PEACOCK	DEC 9	END OF TERM	MAEVE BINCHY
1977	ABBEY	NOV 17	A PAGAN PLACE	EDNA O'BRIEN
1978	PEACOCK	DEC 1	THE HEART'S A WONDER	MAUREEN CHARLTON
1979	PEACOCK	OCT 16	THE NIGHTINGALE AND NOT THE LARK	JENNIFER JOHNSTON
1979	PEACOCK	OCT 22	HALF-PROMISED LAND	MAEVE BINCHY
1979	PEACOCK	SEP 11	OPEN-ENDED PRESCIPTION	LELAND BARDWELL
1980	PEACOCK	-	-	-
1981	PEACOCK	JUN 15	ISLAND PROTECTED BY A BRIDGE OF GLASS	GARRY HYNES
1981	PEACOCK	JUN 17	BAR AND GER	GERALDINE ARON
1981	PEACOCK	DEC 14	THE CAT'S OPERA	EILIS DILLON
1982	PEACOCK	MAY 31	HERE ARE LADIES	SIOBHAN MCKENNA
1982	PEACOCK	JUN 7	ALL JOYCE	SIOBHAN MCKENNA
1983	PEACOCK	NOV 15	MARY MAKEBELIEVE	ROSALEEN LINEHAN/ FERGUS LINEHAN
1983	PEACOCK	JAN 25	SYLVIA PLATH - LETTERS HOME	ROSE GOLDENBERG
1983	PEACOCK	MAY 17	CHOCOLATE CAKE	MARY GALLAGHER
1984	PEACOCK	MAR 8	PROSE AND POETRY	NIAMH MCANALLY
1984	PEACOCK	MAR 20	CRIMES OF THE HEART	BETH HENLEY
1984	PEACOCK	MAY 19	I DO LIKE TO BE BESIDE THE SEASIDE (REHEARSED READING)	ANNE HARTIGAN
1984	PEACOCK	OCT 9	CUIRT AN MHEAN OICHE	SIOBHAN MCKENNA

YEAR	VENUE	DATE	TITLE	PLAYWRIGHT
1985	PEACOCK	JAN 22	FREUD	LYNN ROTH
1985	PEACOCK	JUN 16	LEAMH FILIOCHTA	AINE NI GHLINN
1985	PEACOCK	JUN 16	NO BOGHAISINI GO BRACH	POILIN MCGONIGLE
1985	PEACOCK	JUN 23	AN FEAR SIUIL	LADY GREGORY
1985	PEACOCK	JUN 23	AGALLAMH BEIRTE TA'S AGAM	MAIREAD MACIOMAIRE
1986	PEACOCK	DEC 1	OR BY APPOINTMENT	MAY CLUSKEY
1987	PEACOCK	JUL 20	LADY G	CAROLYN SWIFT
1987	PEACOCK	SEP 28	THE INVISIBLE MAN	JENNIFER JOHNSTON
1987	PEACOCK	DEC 28	SOMEWHERE OVER THE BALCONY	MARIE JONES
1988	PEACOCK	MAY 16	SHADY LADIES	MARY HALPIN
1988	ABBEY	SEP 26	COLOURS	JEAN BINNIE
1988	PEACOCK	NOV 3	DARK LADY	KAREN SUNDE
1988	PEACOCK	NOV 10	O ANANIAS, AZARIAS AND MISAEL	JENNIFER JOHNSTON
1989	PEACOCK	FEB 14	FRAGMENTS OF ISABELLA	ISABELLA LEITNER/ GABRIELLE REIDY
1989	PEACOCK	MAR 2	TRIPTYCH	JENNIFER JOHNSTON
1989	PEACOCK	APR 18	SHADES OF A JELLY WOMAN	JEAN DOYLE/ PETER SHERIDAN
1990	PEACOCK	MAY 30	ULYSSES IN NIGHTTOWN	MARJORIE BARKENTINE
1991	PEACOCK	NOV 19	HOWLING MOONS, SILENT SONS	DEIRDRE HINES
1991	PEACOCK	MAR 19	ULLALOO	MARINA CARR

REHEARSED READINGS OF 'PLAYS BY WOMEN'

YEAR	VENUE	DATE	TITLE	PLAYWRIGHT
1991	PEACOCK	JUN 24	THE WILDE CIRCUS SHOW	IVY BANNISTER
1991	PEACOCK	JUN 27	FIND THE LADY	LOUISE HERMANA
1991	PEACOCK	JUNE 25	DERVOGILLA & HYACINTH HALVEY	LADY GREGORY

YEAR	VENUE	DATE	TITLE	PLAYWRIGHT

REHEARSED READINGS OF 'PLAYS BY WOMEN' IN ASSOC. WITH WOMEN PLAYWRIGHT'S FORUM

YEAR	VENUE	DATE	TITLE	PLAYWRIGHT
1991	PEACOCK	JUN 29	GENERATIONS	COLETTE CONNOR
1991	PEACOCK	JUN 29	BODIES	CLAIRR O'CONNOR
1991	PEACOCK	JUN 29	TWO GIRLS IN SILK KIMONOS	CELIA DE FREINE
1991	PEACOCK	JUN 29	JOCASTA	LELAND BARDWELL
1991	PEACOCK	JUN 29	THE REBEL COUNTESS	IVY BANNISTER
1992	PEACOCK	FEB 6	AWAY ALONE	JANET NOBLE
1992	PEACOCK	JUN 15	BOLD GIRLS	RONA MUNRO
1993	PEACOCK	-	-	-
1994	PEACOCK	SEP 16	THE WALL (REHEARSED READING)	IVY BANNISTER
1994	PEACOCK	SEP 29	THE MAI	MARINA CARR
1994	PEACOCK	NOV 9	DUN NO MBAN TRI THINE	EILIS NI DHUIBHNE
1995	PEACOCK	MAY 30	SMALL CITY	CLARE DOWLING
1995	PEACOCK	OCT 24	PLAYGIRL	KATY HAYES
1996	PEACOCK	MAR 21	PORTIA COUGHLAN	MARINA CARR
1996	PEACOCK	MAY 22	A WING AND A PRAYER	THE BALCONY BELLES
1997	PEACOCK	JUN 24	A DIFFERENT RHYME	LORRAINE O'BRIEN
1998	ABBEY	OCT 1	BY THE BOG OF CATS	MARINA CARR
1999	ABBEY	-	-	-
2000	PEACOCK	APR 5	TREE HOUSES	ELIZABETH KUTI
2001	PEACOCK	MAY 24	THE MEMORY OF WATER	SHELAGH STEPHENSON
2002	PEACOCK	AUG 16	DOLDRUM BAY (READING)	HILARY FANNIN
2002	PEACOCK	AUG 17	LOVERS REUNITED	SIOFRA CAMPBELL
2002	ABBEY	SEP 27	ARIEL	MARINA CARR
2003	PEACOCK	JAN 22	MEAT AND SALT	MARINA CARR
2003	PEACOCK	MAY 7	DOLDRUM BAY	HILARY FANNIN
2003	PEACOCK	SEP 30	DUCK	STELLA FEEHILY
2003	PEACOCK	DEC 10	THE WOLF OF WINTER	PAULA MEEHAN
2004	PEACOCK	SEP 30	PORTIA COUGHLAN	MARINA CARR

WHILE EVERY ATTEMPT WAS MADE TO COMPLETE A COMPREHENSIVE LISTING OF WOMEN PLAYWRIGHTS AT THE ABBEY 1904-2004, INEVITABLY, THERE ARE OMISSIONS. SOME NAMES, DATES AND TITLES OF PLAYS REMAINED ELUSIVE. SOME PLAYS THAT MAY OR MAY NOT HAVE RECEIVED REHEARSED READINGS AT ONE TIME OR ANOTHER ARE NOT LISTED. THE AREA OF RESEARCH IS SO VAST AND AS YET UNTRAMMELLED THAT IT WAS NOT POSSIBLE FOR THE PURPOSES OF THIS PROJECT TO LOCATE ALL OF THE WOMEN WHO PUT WORDS UPON A PAGE AND PLACED THEM ONSTAGE AT THE ABBEY.

COLETTE CONNOR
© 1993, 2009

SELECTED BIBLIOGRAPHY:

CHAMBERS, COLIN, ED., (1995), 'MAKING PLAYS' – THE WRITER-DIRECTOR RELATIONSHIP IN THE THEATRE TODAY. RICHARD NELSON AND DAVID JONES, LONDON, FABER AND FABER

COXHEAD, ELIZABETH, 'LADY GREGORY', MACMILLAN, 1961.

GREGORY, AUGUSTA, 'OUR IRISH THEATRE', AUTOBIOGRAPHY.

HUNT, HUGH (1979), 'THE ABBEY' – IRELAND'S NATIONAL THEATRE 1904-1979, DUBLIN, GILL AND MACMILLAN.

KEARNEY, EILEEN (1991), 'CURRENT WOMEN'S VOICES IN IRISH THEATRE, NEW DRAMATIC VISIONS, DECEMBER 1991, U.S. COLBY QUARTERLY.

KEYSSAR, HELENE (1984), 'FEMINIST THEATRE' – AN INTRODUCTION TO PLAYS OF CONTEMPORARY BRITISH AND AMERICAN WOMEN, LONDON, THE MACMILLAN PRESS LTD.

LEENEY, CATHY (1995) 'THEMES OF RITUAL AND MYTH IN 3 PLAYS BY TERESA DEEVY', IRISH UNIVERSITY REVIEW, SILVER JUBILEE ISSUE, SPRING/SUMMER, 1995.

MCCULLY, KARIN (1996), NATIONAL THEATRE – THE STATE OF THE ABBEY, IN BORT, EBERHARD (ED)., 'STATE OF PLAY – IRISH THEATRE IN THE NINETIES', TURBINGEN, S.GERMAN. CDE STUDIES.

MCMULLAN, ANNA (1993), IRISH WOMEN PLAYWRIGHTS SINCE 1958 IN 'BRITISH AND IRISH WOMEN PLAYWRIGHTS SINCE 1958', EDS. GRIFFITHS, TREVOR R. & LLEWELLYN JONES, MARGARET. BUCKS & PHILADELPHIA, OPEN UNVIVERSITY PRESS.

MURRAY, CHRISTOPHER, (1995), 'THE STIFLED VOICE', INTRODUCTION, IRISH UNIVERSITY REVIEW, SILVER JUBILEE ISSUE, VOL.25. NO.1. SPRING/SUMMER, 1995.

O'DONNELL, MARY (1991), WOMEN AT THE PEACOCK: 'READINGS FOR WOMEN PLAYWRIGHTS – BUT WHY NOT FULL PRODUCTIONS?' DUBLIN. IRISH TIMES, JULY 4TH 1991.

ROCHE, ANTHONY, (1994), 'CONTEMPORARY IRISH DRAMA' – FROM BECKETT TO MCGUINNESS, DUBLIN, GILL AND MACMILLAN.

SHEEHY, KAY (1994), 'FEW CURTAINS RISE FOR WOMEN', INTERVIEW WITH GARRY HYNES, IRISH TIMES, MAY 11TH, 1994, P.11.

SMITH, AILBHE, ED. (1992), 'WILDISH THINGS' – AN ANTHOLOGY OF NEW IRISH WOMEN'S WRITING, DUBLIN, ATTIC PRESS.

WANDOR, MICHELINE (1981), 'UNDERSTUDIES' – THEATRE AND SEXUAL POLITICS, LONDON, EYRE METHUEN.

WHITE, VICTORIA, (1992), 'THERE ARE NO WOMEN PLAYWRIGHTS', IRISH TIMES, JULY 1ST, 1992.

WOOLF, VIRGINIA, (1945), 'A ROOM OF ONE'S OWN', PENGUIN, LONDON & U.S.A.

Abbey Theatre.

1906/7

NATIONAL THEATRE SOCIETY LIMITED.
SPECIAL SATURDAY-
NIGHT PERFORMANCES.

The Directors of the National Theatre Society have the honour to announce that they have arranged for the production of a series of Plays which will be given on Ten Saturday Evenings, at 8.15, during the months of October, November, December and January.

The Plays to be produced are as follows:—

Sat. Oct. 20th.

First Production of THE GAOL GATE, a Tragedy in one Act, by Lady Gregory. First Production of THE MINERAL WORKERS, a Play in Three Acts, by William Boyle. SPREADING THE NEWS, a Comedy in One Act, by Lady Gregory.

Sat. Nov. 10th.

RIDERS TO THE SEA, a Play in One Act, by J. M. Synge. THE DOCTOR IN SPITE OF HIMSELF, a Comedy in Three Acts, by Molière; translated by Lady Gregory. HYACINTH HALVEY, a Comedy in One Act, by Lady Gregory.

Sat. Nov. 17th.

THE ELOQUENT DEMPSY, a Comedy in Three Acts, by William Boyle. KATHLEEN NI HOULIHAN, a Play in One Act, by W. B. Yeats.

Sat. Nov. 24th.

First production of DEIRDRE, a Play in verse, by W. B. Yeats. First production of THE CANAVANS, a Play in Three Acts, by Lady Gregory.

Sat. Dec. 8th.

THE HOUR GLASS, a morality in One Act, by W. B. Yeats. THE BUILDING FUND, a Comedy in Three Acts, by William Boyle. THE POORHOUSE, a Comedy, by Lady Gregory and Dr. Douglas Hyde.

Sat. Dec. 15th.

IN THE SHADOW OF THE GLEN, a Play in One Act, by J. M. Synge. THE WHITE COCKADE, an Historical Play in Three Acts, by Lady Gregory.

Sat. Dec. 29th.

First production of THE PLAYBOY OF THE WESTERN WORLD, a Play in Three Acts, by J. M. Synge.

Sat. Jan. 12th, 1907.

ON BAILE'S STRAND, a Play in verse, by W. B. Yeats. HYACINTH HALVEY, a Comedy in one Act, by Lady Gregory. THE RISING OF THE MOON, a Play in One Act, by Lady Gregory.

Sat. Jan. 19th.

First production of THE PLEADERS, a Comedy in Five Acts, by Racine, translated from the French.

Sat. Jan. 26th.

THE ANTIGONE OF SOPHOCLES, translated by Robert Gregory. First production of FAND, a Play in verse in Two Acts, by Wilfred Scawen Blunt.

The above list affords a rare opportunity to all lovers of the Drama of studying new Plays by Authors whose works have received high commendation from competent critics ; have been successfully toured in Ireland, Scotland and England, and some of which have been played in Germany, Bohemia and America.

In order to draw the attention of the general public to the work done by the Society, the Directors have arranged for the issue of

SPECIAL SUBSCRIPTION TICKETS AT A CONSIDERABLE REDUCTION,

AND FOR THE

SUM OF ONE GUINEA A NUMBERED AND RESERVED STALL CAN BE SECURED

for the large number of Plays mentioned on the dates given above. It is hoped that a liberal support will be accorded to this comprehensive scheme, as it may be noted that the list includes seven Plays to be produced for the first time on any Stage, besides several revivals of successful works ; thus enabling playgoers to witness a series of Plays which should be of deep interest to the many who are watching the progress of a school of playwrights in their efforts to establish a *distinctive National Drama in Ireland.*

Attention may also be directed to the translated Plays of Molière and Racine, and the still more interesting experiment of producing one of the masterpieces of Greek Drama—the Antigone of Sophocles.

It is proposed to give in the Abbey Theatre during the winter months a series of Lectures on Dramatic Art, to which all holders of a Subscription Ticket will be invited.

Further information respecting seats, etc., can be had from Messrs. Cramer, Wood & Co., Westmoreland Street. Early application is requested as the seating accommodation is limited.

Signed,

W. A. HENDERSON,

Secretary.

October 12th, 1906.

N.B.—Some changes in the order of production may be necessary—for reasons now unforeseen, but every effort will be made to carry out the list as advertised.

ABBEY THEATRE
— DUBLIN —

Playing at

THE QUEEN'S THEATRE

Monday, 22nd October 1951, and following nights at 7.45

FIRST PRODUCTION OF

WINDOW ON THE SQUARE

A Play in Three Acts by Anne Daly

Characters:

NINETTE DOWNIE	Dóirín Ní Mhaidín
MRS. DOWNIE	Máire Ní Chatháin
LIZ PURDON	Bríd Ní Loinsigh
AMBROSE CREAGH	Eamon Guaillí
ESSIE GOGGIN	Ité Ní Mhathúna
JANIE GOGGIN	Aingeal Ní Nuamain
MATT BREW	Seathrún O Goilí
JOHN PAUL CREAGH	Rae Mac An Ailf
MARCELLA MARIA CREAGH	Siobhán Ní Eaghra
PHILLY DRISCOLL	Micheál O hAonghusa

The action of the play takes place in the drawing-room of Mrs. Downie's house, Market Square, Dromeen.

SMOKING WILL NOT BE PERMITTED IN THE AUDITORIUM

ACT I: Scene I: A winter evening in the year 1900.
        Scene II: Three years later.
ACT II: Scene I: A morning in October, 17 years later.
        Scene II: Evening of the same day.
ACT III: Scene I: Two years later.
        Scene II: Later in the same day.

There will be Intervals of Twelve Minutes between the Acts

Play produced by RIA MOONEY
Setting by ROBERT HEADE
Stage Manager: SEÁN O MAONAIGH

ORCHESTRA

The Orchestra, under the direction of Eamonn O Gallchobhair, will perform the following selections:

Overture	Martha	*Flotow*
Selection from Madame Butterfly		*Puccini*
Ceol Gaolach		*B. O Gallchobhair*

FORTHCOMING PRODUCTIONS

THE SHADOW OF A GUNMAN
By Seán O'Casey

VILLAGE WOOING
By Bernard Shaw

INNOCENT BYSTANDER
By Séamus Byrne (First Production)

THE NEW GOSSOON
By George Shiels

BARS OPEN DURING INTERVALS AND FOR THIRTY MINUTES AFTER PERFORMANCE

LIFFEY LANE

A Play In Three Acts
By MAURA LAVERTY

CHARACTERS

BILLY QUINLAN	...	...	...	...	SHAY GRENNAN
MRS. DOYLE	...	...	...	...	KATHLEEN MOLLOY
LAR DOYLE	...	...	...	...	ALFRED MURPHY
CHRISSIE DOYLE	...	...	...	...	DEIRDRE WHELAN
CUT-THE-RASHER	...	...	...	...	KATHLEEN AHERN
BRIDIE FANNING	...	...	...	...	FLORENCE MURPHY
JIM SWEENEY	...	...	...	...	AIDAN FOGARTY
NANNIE BUCKLEY	...	...	...	...	EILEEN DELANEY
RINGMAN	...	...	...	...	BILL CHALKLEY
LOOKOUT MAN	...	...	...	...	JACK ROWE
GUARD	...	...	...	...	JIM WOLOHAN
MRS. BUCKLEY'S VOICE	...	...	...	CATHLEEN FINNEGAN

TOSS SCHOOL—PADDY FINNEGAN, PADDY CAHILL, WILLIE MURPHY, PAT McKENNA.

CHILDREN — ANNETTE CHALKLEY, BRENDA CHALKLEY, ANGELA LONG.

COFFEE COUNTER NOW OPEN IN STALLS BAR

PROLOGUE

ACT I: Scene I   Street between the Penny Dinners and the Lane.
      Scene II   The Lane—Evening of the same day.
      Scene III   The Doyle's Room—same evening.
      Scene IV   The Lane—A few minutes later.

ACT II: Scene I   A Dublin street—The day before Hallowe'en.
      Scene II   The Lane, same day—about 7 o'clock.
      Scene III   The Toss School—an hour later.
      Scene IV   The Lane—same evening.

ACT III: Scene I   The Lane—Hallowe'en, about 3 p.m. in the afternoon.
      Scene II   Whitechurch Road. An hour later.
      Scene III   The Lane—a little later.
      Scene IV   The Doyle's Room—a few minutes later.
      Scene V   The Lane—a few minutes later.

★

PRODUCTION —————————— CATHLEEN FINNEGAN

★

There will be Intervals of Ten Minutes between the Acts.

ORCHESTRA

The Orchestra under the direction of Paul Caffrey will perform the following selections:—

OVERTURE—DIE ITALIENEIN IN ALGIER . . . . . ROSSINI
1st INTERVAL—THE SHAMROCK . . . . . MYDDLETON
2nd INTERVAL—DANCE OF THE TUMBLERS . . . . RIMSKY-KORSAKOV
DANCE OF THE FLOWER GIRLS . . . . KHACHATURIAN

SMOKING WILL NOT BE PERMITTED IN THE AUDITORIUM

PLAYS BY WOMEN

PEACOCK THEATRE

June 24th - June 29th

A SERIES OF REHEARSED READINGS

CAST LIST

THE WILDE CIRCUS SHOW
by Ivy Bannister

Reading directed by Mary Elizabeth Burke Kennedy

Monday 24th and Wednesday 26th June

Sir William Wilde	Ray McBride
The Disagreeable Man	Macdara O Fátharta
Speranzo	Joan O'Hara
Mary Travers	Marie Mullen
Constance	Máire Ní Ghráinne
Oscar	Des Cave
Willie	Clive Geraghty
Isola	Paula McFettridge
Beautiful Young Man	Paul Hickey

(There will be an interval of 15 minutes)

FIND THE LADY : THE LIFE OF KATE O'BRIEN
By Louise Hermana
(Developed with the assistance of Nuala Hayes)

Reading directed by Pat Murphy

Thursday 27th and Saturday 29th June

Kate	Fedelma Cullen
Kitty	Paual McFettridge
Constance	Marie Mullen
Philip	MacDara O'Fátharta

(There will be an interval of 15 minutes)

DERVORGILLA and HYACINTH HALVEY
2 One-Acts by Lady Gregory

Readings directed by Judy Friel

Tuesday 25th and Friday 28th

Dervorgilla	Fedelma Cullen
Flann	Des Cave
Mona	Máire Ní Ghráinne
Wandering Songmaker	Macdara O'Fátharta
Mamie	Paula McFetteridge
Owen	Paul Hickey

Miss Delane	Joan O'Hara
Mr Quirke	Clive Geraghty
Faherty Farrell	Paul Hickey
Miss Joyce	Máire Ní Ghráinne
Sergeant	Macdara O'Fátharta
Hyacinth Halvey	Des Cave

(There will be no interval)

Lighting	Tony Wakefield
Stage Director	Mairead McGrath
Stage Manager	John Kells
Sound	Dave O'Brien
Assistant Stage Manager	Micil Ryan

WOMEN PLAYWRIGHTS FORUM

On Saturday 29th June, the Peacock Theatre will host an
all-day series of readings from the plays of five Irish
women playwrights, Colette O'Connor, Clairr O'Connor, Celia
deFreine, Leland Bardwell, Ivy Bannister. The readings
will be followed by a forum on women and playwrighting.

Saturday 29 June

MORNING   11.00 - 1.00

11.00   GENERATIONS   By Colette O'Connor

Laura Hayden   Kate Thompson
Peter Hayden   Conor Mullen
Roz Hayden   Katrina Shine
Michael Chambers   Jim Reid
Harry Baker   Malcolm Douglas
Bea Bentine   Jill Doyle
Director   Claire Wilson

12.00   BODIES   By Clairr O'Connor

Beth   Clodagh O'Donoghue
Ní   James Barry
Uncle Joe   Mark Searon
Aunt Sal   Roisin Flood
Ann   Frances Coghlan
Thin Girl   Pauline Shanahan
Bishop   Hugh Hartigan
Vincent   Jim Culleton
Stage Manager   Pamela Scully
Director   Cathy Leeney

1.00   Lunch

Coffee and sandwiches available in Foyer

AFTERNOON   2.00 - 6.00

2.00   TWO GIRLS IN SILK KIMONOS   By Celia de Freine

Constance Markiewicz   Nuala Hayes
Eva Gore Booth   Helen Norton
Flute and other parts   Ellen Cranitch
Maeve Markiewicz and other parts   Deirdre Molloy
Double Bass and other parts   Sean Gormley
Director   Máire O'Higgins

```
3.00            JOCASTA                By Leland Bardwell

Jocaste                                Liz  Lloyd
Laius                                  David O'Brien
Creon                                  David Heap
Sophocles                              William Byrne
Oedipus                                Lorcan Cranitch
Teiresias                              Frank O'Sullivan
Chorus                                 Siobhan Miley
Other Parts                            Risteard Cooper
Director                               Mia Gallagher

                ─────────────

4.00    Coffee

                ─────────────

4.30       THE REBEL COUNTESS          By Ivy Bannister

Con                                    Ruth Hegarty
Countess                               Blanaid Irvine
Count                                  Sean Campion
Director                               Caroline FirzGerald

                ─────────────

5.00 - 6.00     Discussion of Five Plays and of the Place
                of Women Playwrights in Today's Theatre.

                Chaired by Phyl Herbert
```